The Nature of the Atonement

The Nature of the Atonement

James Morison

Copyright © Scripture Teaching Library, 2014.

ISBN: 978-1-909789-19-7

All rights reserved. No part of this publication may be reproduced, stored in or introduced into a retrieval system, or transmitted, in any form or by any means (electronic, mechanical, photocopying, recording or otherwise), without the prior written permission of the copyright owner.

Published by
SCRIPTURE TEACHING LIBRARY
Cookstown, Northern Ireland.

www.scriptureteachinglibrary.com

Printed by Kingsbridge Press Ltd, Cookstown, Northern Ireland.

Cover image: 'The Scapegoat' by William Holman Hunt (1827–1910), Wikimedia Commons

Preface

THIS BRIEF TREATISE on *The Nature of the Atonement* was first issued at a very early stage in my ministry. Edition after edition was called for, while proofs multiplied that it was being blessed to many. Several years ago it went out of print, and since that time I have been repeatedly urged to reissue it. My purpose was to rewrite and enlarge. As, however, the pressure to reissue it in its original form has been increased of late, I have yielded. Some slight alterations have been made, but the style and argument are as at first.

J. Morison,
Florentine Bank House,
Glasgow,
April, 1890.

Contents

1 Introduction   9

2 The Atonement Not Pardon   13

3 The Atonement Not Justification   25

4 The Atonement Not Redemption   35

5 The Atonement Not Reconciliation   47

6 The Atonement Not Payment of Debt   61

7 The Atonement: What It Is   75

8 Notes   93

Except where otherwise indicated, all quotations from Scripture are taken from the Authorised (King James) Version.

Introduction

'Jesus Christ is the propitiation for our sins.'

2 John 2:2.

THE WHOLE VERSE in which these words occur is as follows: 'Jesus Christ is the propitiation for our sins; and not for ours only, but also for [the sins of] the whole world.'

Perhaps our readers would be glad were we to proceed immediately to discuss the all-engrossing subject referred to in the last clause of the verse.

No subject, certainly, could excel that in interest. It comes home to the heart; for it is a matter of life and death to every man to ascertain whether or not he be warranted to say, 'Jesus loved *me*, and gave Himself for *me*.'

We must, however, for the present, confine our own attention, and that of our readers, to the first clause of the verse, 'He is the propitiation for our sins.'

The word *propitiation* is equivalent to the word *atonement*. The two terms are practically synonymous. This either is, or ought to be, admitted by all. The same Greek word that is rendered *propitiation* in 1 John 2:2 is used in exactly the same sense in 1 John 4:10: 'Herein is love, not that we loved God, but that He loved us, and sent His Son to be the *propitiation* for our sins.'

The apostle Paul uses a kindred expression, in exactly the same sense, in Romans 3:25: 'Whom God set forth [propitiatory or] a *propitiation* through faith in His blood, to declare His righteousness for the remission of sins that are past, through the forbearance of God; to declare, I say, at this time His righteousness, that He might be just, and the justifier of him who believeth in Jesus.'

The apostle says propitiatory, or *propitiation*, rather than *propitiator*, because Christ was Himself the sacrifice, as well as the sacrificer; and it is the victim-lamb of God, as such, that the sinner is to behold taking away [or bearing] the sin of the world. (Jn 1:29).

In Hebrews 2:17, moreover, the verb, of which this is the noun, occurs in exactly the same sense; for there the expression, 'to make reconciliation', is of precisely the same import with the phrase, 'to make atonement'. In discussing therefore this great theme we shall, for the most part, use indifferently the words, *propitiation* and *atonement*.

What, then, is the atonement?

This is the question to the answer of which we address ourselves.

Chapter One

The Atonement Not Pardon

They differ entirely the one from the other.

(1) This difference may be thus exhibited: *Pardon comes to us immediately upon confession of sin, and hence thereafter; whereas the atonement was made for all of us centuries ago.*[*]

Need we prove that pardon comes to us after confession? Take one passage: 'If we confess our sins, God is faithful and just to forgive us our sins, and to cleanse us from all unrighteousness' (1 Jn 1:9). *To forgive sins* is

---

[*] The late eminent United Secession minister, Mr. Ballantyne of Stonehaven, said to a brother minister, a very short time before his death, 'I could have no hope as a sinner, if Christ did not die for all men.' It is thus that I, too, feel.

just *to pardon sins*. The word *forgive* might have been rendered *pardon*. Now, the apostle here says that if we confess our sins, God will pardon them; and, consequently, He must be understood to intimate that our sins unconfessed remain unforgiven. Confession is thus a pre-requisite to pardon. It cannot, however, in our case, that is, in this age of the world, go before the propitiation, for the propitiation was something effected more than eighteen hundred years ago, when, on the cross, the expiring and exulting Saviour exclaimed, 'It is finished'. Do we need to prove that the propitiation was then completed? Read one passage, Hebrews 9:26: 'Now once (for all) in the end of the world [that is, at the close of the Mosaic Dispensation, eighteen hundred years ago], hath Christ appeared to put away sin, [that is, to make atonement for sin] by the sacrifice of Himself.'

The atonement, then, and pardon must be two very different blessings, for the atonement now precedes, whereas pardon follows confession of sin.

(2) The difference between the two blessings may be exhibited thus: *We pray for pardon, but not for the atonement.* All saints pray for pardon. Saints under the Old Testament prayed for it. Observe the 'man

greatly beloved,' Daniel. Take note of his remarkable prayer, recorded in the ninth chapter of the book which goes by his name. In the nineteenth verse he winds up his confessions and intercessions by saying, 'O Lord, hear; O Lord, *forgive* [that is, *pardon*]; O Lord, hearken and do; defer not for Thine own sake, O my God; for Thy city and Thy people are called by Thy name.'

Saints under the New Testament also pray for pardon; for saints delight to obey Christ, and Christ has taught us in His pattern of prayer, to say, 'forgive us [pardon us] our debts, as we forgive our debtors.' Saints, moreover, delight to walk in the footsteps of the Lord's apostles; and Peter admonished Simon Magus to 'repent, and pray God, if perhaps the thought of his heart might be forgiven him' (Acts 8:22). But while saints pray for pardon, in this age of the world, they do not pray for atonement. It is praise and not prayer that is the appropriate exercise here. Were we to pray for it, we should be guilty of unbelief; for our petitions would be a virtual denial of the accomplished fact. The propitiation and pardon, then, must be 'things that differ'; for the one is in every age a proper subject of prayer, the other is not.

(3) The propitiation is not pardon, for *God pardons often, whereas the propitiation was but*

once made. Does not God pardon often? Ah! woe to ever-sinning man, if He did not. But He does. Our Saviour taught His disciples to pray daily for pardon. This we prove by the same pattern of prayer already referred to. That is a prayer to be presented daily. One petition in it is, 'give us *this day* our daily bread.' Now, then, it is our duty to pray, 'forgive us our debts, as we forgive our debtors.' In other words, we need new pardon every day. And there is new pardon for us every day. Hence, Daniel says (9:9), 'To the Lord our God belong mercies and forgivenesses'; and Nehemiah (9:17) appeals to God, and says, 'But thou art a God ready to pardon,' or, as it is in the original and margin, 'a God of pardons.' God is not, however, a God of propitiations. The propitiation accomplished on Calvary is never to be repeated. It already extends its 'exceeding breadth' over all the sins that ever have, or ever shall be committed. Were it to be multiplied, its multiplication would be a stigma on itself; for it would be a refutation of its own infinite value. Scripture asserts most clearly that the propitiation is ONE, and but ONCE made. Paul says, 'Christ being raised from the dead, dieth no more; death hath no more dominion over Him; for in that He died, He died unto sin ONCE' (Rom. 6:9, 10). He says again, contrasting Jesus with the Levitical high-priests, 'He needeth not daily, as those high-priests, to offer up sacrifice, first for His own sins, and then for the people's; for this He did ONCE, when He offered up Himself' (Heb. 7:27). He says again, 'Christ was ONCE offered to bear the sins of many' (Heb. 9:28). He says again, 'This man, after He had offered ONE sacrifice for sins, for ever sat down on the right hand of God' (Heb. 10:12). He warns his Christian readers to 'hold fast the profession of their faith'; 'for if we sin wilfully,' says he, 'after that we have received the knowledge of the truth, there remaineth *no more sacrifice* for sins' (Heb. 10:26). The apostle Peter likewise tells us, that 'Christ hath ONCE suffered for sins, the just for the unjust, that He might bring us to God' (1 Pet. 3:18). Seeing, then, that it is true, that the propitiation is but once made, whereas pardon is capable of almost indefinite multiplication, it is very manifest that the one must be radically and essentially a different thing from the other.

(4) The propitiation is not pardon, because *God bestows pardon, whereas He receives the propitiation.* Pardon is something granted by God; the propitiation is something made to God. The truth of this distinction cannot but flash upon the mind of every intelligent

person. A single portion of Scripture is sufficient to establish both branches of the affirmation: that portion is found in Leviticus 4:20. In the context, the Lord is stating the provision He had appointed for the pardon of a 'sin through ignorance,' committed by 'the whole congregation of Israel.' He enjoins them to 'offer a young bullock for the sin'; and He orders that the priest 'shall do with the bullock, as he did with the bullock for a sin-offering, so shall he do with this; and the priest shall make an atonement for them, and it shall be forgiven them.' (See also verses 26, 31, 35.) Now, here we have, in the typical dispensation, the victim offered up as an atonement made *to* God; and, consequent upon this, we have the forgiveness or pardon vouchsafed *by* God. (See Eph. 4:32; 5:2). Pardon and propitiation therefore are two very different things.

(5) The propitiation is not pardon, because it is *Christ alone that propitiates, whereas it is, when properly speaking, God the Father that pardons*. No argument is needed to show that it is not God the Father, but God the Son, that makes propitiation. It is 'Jesus Christ the righteous' Who is 'the propitiation for our sins.' It is Immanuel, the incarnate God, that 'purchased the church with His own blood' (Acts 20:28). It is equally

manifest that it is properly God the Father, and not God the Son, that bestows pardon. It is true, seeing the Son and the Father 'are ONE' (Jn 10:30), that the Son may, in language that is popular, and not strictly philosophical, be said to pardon. He is 'exalted a Prince and a Saviour, to give repentance unto Israel, and *forgiveness of sins*' (Acts 5:31). 'The Son of Man hath power on earth to *forgive sins*' (Matt. 9:6; see also Col. 3:13). Still, however, it is beyond contradiction that it is the Father, properly speaking, who forgives. Hence the Saviour taught His disciples to pray to God, 'their Father and His Father,' to 'forgive their debts, as they forgave their debtors' (Matt. 6:12; see also Matt. 6:14, 15; 18:35, &c.). Hence the Saviour Himself prays to the Father on the cross, 'Father, forgive them; for they know not what they do' (Lk 23:34). And by turning to the last verse of the fourth chapter of the epistle to the Ephesians, we perceive the strictly accurate manner of stating the operation of Deity in this matter: 'Be ye kind one to another, tenderhearted, forgiving one another, even as *God for Christ's sake* hath forgiven you,' or, as it is in the Revised Version, 'Even as God also in Christ forgave you.' Seeing, then, it is Christ alone Who atones, and seeing it is God the Father Who is properly said to pardon, it is evident that propitiation and pardon must be two things essentially different.

(6) Atonement is not pardon, because *pardon has reference to God's character as a Father, whereas the propitiation has reference to His character as a Moral Governor.* Confusion on this subject engenders confusion on many others connected with sin and salvation. It is of the utmost importance to make the necessary and scriptural discrimination between the fatherly and the rectoral character of God. Now, it is in His fatherly, and not in His judicial character, that He pardons. A judge (who is always, in human governments, merely the representative of the supreme governor) cannot pardon. In his private character (that is, as a man and neighbour) he may pardon a personal offence, or a thousand offences; but in his public character (that is, as a judge) he must be just. He is, in this character; competent only to give expression to the law. He is the law's mouth, and can say nothing which the law does not say. Law never makes, and cannot, in the nature of things, make provision for pardon. When a criminal receives pardon, it is not from the judge, it is not from the lawgiver as such, it is not from the supreme ruler as the administrator of

public justice, but it is from the supreme ruler as *father of the people.* Pardon is essentially extra-judicial, extra-rectoral. Now, it is in God's character as Father, and in that alone, that He pardons. Hence, when we pray to Him for pardon, we pray to Him as 'our Father.' Hence, also, it is necessary that the self-same sins which have already been fully atoned for, be also pardoned, before we can enjoy the smilings of 'our Father's' countenance. Propitiation is thus a thing essentially different from pardon. It has exclusive reference to God's rectoral character. God needs no 'propitiation' as a Father and a 'Friend'; but as the Moral Ruler, and Guardian of the public weal, He must maintain the efficacy of His laws and the stability of His government; and, consequently, 'He can by no means clear the guilty,' without an expedient that will as effectually secure the public welfare as the everlasting perdition of the transgressors themselves. In other words, He must have an atonement. The propitiation thus has reference to sin, as an act of disobedience towards God as our Governor; whereas pardon has reference to sin, as an act of filial ingratitude toward our tender-hearted 'Abba, Father.' Hence it is, that the same sins must both be atoned for and pardoned, before we can enjoy at once the rectoral and fatherly favour of God.'*

Some seem to suppose that, by the death of Christ, all the sins of all men have been pardoned, except the sin of unbelief; and they sometimes express themselves in a manner calculated to convey the impression, that no sin but the sin of unbelief will be laid to the charge of the finally impenitent. This idea is quite an erroneous view of the atonement of Christ. It is laden with insuperable difficulties. In the first place, it expressly contradicts the Scriptures; for we are there told that other sins, beside that of unbelief, will incur penalty in the place of doom (Rev. 21:8, Eph. 5:3, 6). In the second place, it gives no satisfactory reason why, when all other sins are atoned for, unbelief should be excluded. In the third place, it would involve, as a necessary consequence, the final ruin of almost all believers. Most believers are, at some period of their life or

---

* It is by overlooking the distinction between these two characters which God sustains toward us that Socinians and Priestleyans (the *soi-disant* Unitarians) deny the necessity of an atonement. They tell us that a benevolent parent needs no 'bloody sacrifice' to induce him to pardon an offending child. They mock 'the remorseless God of the Calvinists.' But when was a judge abused even by them because he was rigidly just, in denouncing the penalty of the law against his own child, who had become a public criminal!

another, guilty of the sin of unbelief; and if there were no provision for its pardon in the death of Christ, of the same nature with the provision for the pardon of other sins, their salvation would be as impossible as the salvation of beings, for the pardon of whose sins there is no provision at all. In the fourth place, it would also involve, as a necessary consequence, but in antagonism to the teaching of Scripture, the idea of the final salvation of the whole heathen world, and not simply, as Paul tells us, of those who 'Do by nature the things contained in the law' (Rom. 2:13–15). If this were true, how cruel to send the gospel to the Indies and 'the isles'! How unmerciful to obey our Saviour, and 'go into all the world, and preach the gospel to every creature'! How happy to be 'without God in the world'! How unhappy to be born in a Christian land! What a pity that the 'good news' should ever be made known to any till after death!

It is true, indeed – and where is the heart that does not beat high with gratitude because it is true? – that there is no sin but unbelief standing between the sinner and salvation. Nothing but unbelief will keep a gospel hearer out of heaven. His thefts will not; his lies will not; his drunkenness will not; his oaths will not; his love of sin will not;

his hatred of holiness will not; his past unbelief itself will not. It is his present unbelief alone that keeps him from pardon. If he finally perish, this, and this only, will be his 'condemnation' – 'he hath not believed in the name of the only begotten Son of God' (Jn 3:18, 19). But whilst all this is blessed truth, most precious gospel, it is very different from saying that all sins, except unbelief, have been pardoned. The death of Christ, in itself, cancelled no sin. It opened up the way for the pardon of any and every sin. The death of Christ, as the great and good Archbishop Usher says, 'only makes the sins of mankind fit for pardon.' It has effected an expedient, in consideration of which all sins may, and without which no sin could be, pardoned. Unbelief itself has been atoned for. It is not, as being unatoned for, but as rejective of the atonement made for it, that it ruins the soul; and it, with every other sin, will be blotted out of the book of God's remembrance, the moment that a man 'believes in his heart, and confesses with his mouth,' the truth as it is in Jesus (Rom. 10:9).

The propitiation, then, is not pardon. It is an expedient introduced into the divine moral government, in consideration of which every sin may be pardoned. It is the judicial ground of pardon.

Chapter Two

The Atonement Not Justification

WE DO NOT KNOW if there be a single individual in Christendom who would, in so many words, aver the identity of the propitiation and justification. There was once a class of religionists, pretty extensively scattered over England, and, we suppose, also in Scotland, who held that all the elect were justified at Christ's resurrection.[*] A modification of this opinion is found in the theory of those who attribute to that event in the Saviour's history only the 'fundamental

---

[*] Some even held that they were justified from all eternity. This strange opinion was maintained, and elaborately defined, by Richard Thomson, whose work on the subject was in 1618 learnedly answered by Robert Abbot, Bishop of Salisbury.

justification' of those of whom He was the representative. Whilst there may be few who now subscribe to such scholastic doctrines, it is not unlikely that there is in many minds a latent undefined confounding of the propitiation and justification. Moreover, it is from a secret confusion of these two very different ideas that many entertain a dread of the theory of a universal propitiation. They really define the propitiation as justification ought to be defined; and, bearing this definition of the propitiation in mind, they cannot but attach the idea of heresy to its alleged universality. There are, also, not a few, who are advocates of the unlimited propitiation, who do nearly identify it with what justification really is, when it is properly defined, and who thus find themselves and their theory besieged by a host of formidable objections. But whatever the propitiation, and whatever justification may be, they cannot possibly be one and the same. This is rendered clear by the following considerations:

(1) *The propitiation is something made by Christ, whereas justification is an act of God the Father.* It is 'Jesus Christ' Who is 'the propitiation for the sins of the whole world' (1 Jn 2:2). It is God, the Father of Jesus, Who,

through the propitiation of Christ, is 'just, and the *justifier* of him who believeth' (Rom. 3:26).

(2) *The propitiation was 'finished' many ages ago, whereas justification takes place now, and comes after believing.* It has already been amply shown that it is centuries ago since the propitiation was completed on Calvary; and in order to demonstrate that justification invariably comes after believing, we need only refer to that one typical passage in the apostle's Epistle to the Romans, 'A man is justified by faith' (Rom. 3:28). Thus justification follows faith, and the propitiation is the prior object contemplated by faith. The propitiation is presupposed in faith, whereas justification presupposes faith.

(3) *The propitiation is a general blessing, out of which all believers draw their personal salvation; whereas justification is a special blessing, which cannot serve more than one individual.* One man's justification cannot serve for another man. But the same propitiation which serves one, serves others also. Justification is multiplied with the number of the believers; the propitiation is ever and only ONE.

(4) *The propitiation is spoken of in Scripture as a thing that is past, whereas justification is sometimes spoken of as a future blessing.* As to the former, it is said, 'Christ gave Himself a ransom for all' (1 Tim. 2:6). As to the latter, it is

said, 'It is one God which shall justify the circumcision by faith, and the uncircumcision through faith' (Rom. 3:30). 'By His knowledge,' (see. Phil. 3:8,) says the complacent Father, after the completion of the work given Christ to do, 'shall my righteous servant justify many,' for He hath borne their iniquities' (Isa. 53:11).

It is thus abundantly evident, that whatever justification may be, and whatever the propitiation may be, they cannot possibly be one and the same. If, then, any one, whether he be an adherent of the limited or of the unlimited view of the propitiation, so define that doctrine as to describe justification, that view of the propitiation must be but a denizen and a fancy of his own mind. We have heard persons talking of the propitiation as if it were the deliverance of the elect from the condemnation of the Law. Others have been heard asserting that Christ, by His death, delivered all men from the condemnation of the Law. Both of these parties, though differing in their views of the extent of the propitiation, are at one in their views of its nature; and both of them are quite beside the truth Christ's death, in itself considered, delivered neither all men in general, nor the elect in particular, from the condemnation of the Law. Deliverance from the condemnation of the Law is justification and not the atonement.

Is it possible, then, to prove that it is JUSTIFICATION, which means deliverance from the condemnation of the Law? Clearly so. And yet it is of importance that we should understand that justification is not pardon. It is indeed not infrequently, though improperly confounded with it. It is indeed substantially the same blessing. It is implied in pardon, (Rom. 4:6–8; see also Matt. 9:2; 26:28; Acts 5:31; 26:18, etc.). But then it is the same blessing, viewed in quite a peculiar aspect, and imparted to us by God in quite a different relation from that which He sustains when He pardons. This will be at once evident when we reflect that the same individual may be *often* pardoned though he be only *once* justified.

Moreover, God pardons only as a Father; whereas He justifies only in His character of Judge. Justification is a forensic word. Sin when being pardoned is contemplated as an act of filial disobedience. Sin cannot be justified; and when the sinner receives justification his sins are regarded as transgressions of the public law.

Justification, then, is not to be confounded with pardon. But this is only saying what it is not. The question still recurs, What, then, is it? Is it really *the deliverance of the believer from the condemnation of the Law?* It is. This will appear evident if we remember that justification is the natural opposite of condemnation.* The two terms are antipodes. This is made manifest by many passages of Scripture. Take the following examples: 'They shall *justify* the righteous, and *condemn* the wicked' (Deut. 25:1). 'If I *justify* myself,' says Job, 'mine own mouth shall *condemn* me' (Job 9:20). 'He that *justifieth* the wicked, and he that *condemneth* the just, even they both are abomination to the Lord' (Prov. 17:15). There is also an important passage in Romans 5:16, showing the same contrast: 'The judgement was by one [offence] to *condemnation,* but the free gift is of many offences unto *justification*' (see also Rom. 8:33, 34). Justification is then the exact opposite of condemnation. It is that which, in the case of the sinner, negatives and neutralises condemnation. In human courts of judicature, a condemned criminal cannot afterwards be justified. He may be pardoned, but he cannot be justified. It is different, however, in the relation of the sinner to the law and the gospel. Every sinner

---

* 'The word justify is uniformly the opposite of the word condemn,' says Dr. Anderson, of America, in his treatise on *Justification by Faith.*

is a criminal, and condemned by the Law of God. Every believing sinner is a criminal still, but he is no longer a condemned criminal. By faith he passes out of a state of condemnation into a state of justification. In human courts, justification prevents condemnation. In the court of the gospel, justification presupposes and neutralises condemnation: it delivers from condemnation already incurred. Until a man, however, becomes a believer, he is under condemnation. None 'pass from death unto life' until they believe the truth as it is in Jesus. See John 5:24. All are 'by nature the children of wrath' (Eph. 2:3). Being under the Law, (Rom. 7:4–6), which condemns all, (Rom. 3:19, 20), all are condemned (Rom. 8:1). The Law fulminates its threatenings against all; its curses stand against all; and all this continues till the individual's 'faith is counted for righteousness' (Rom. 4:5); and then, being 'in Christ,' there is 'now no condemnation' to him (Rom. 8:1).

Now we are prepared to answer the question, '*When* is a man delivered from liability to the penalty of the broken Law?' It is only when he believes. The death of Christ, then, did not deliver the unborn elect from the condemnation of the Law. For, if it did, then the elect were justified before they were condemned; and men were treated as sinners and as righteous before they were men. It is plainly evident that the sun does not shine on us at midnight; but this is no more plainly evident than that the elect were not actually liberated from the condemnation of the Law before their actual existence. Manifestly, then, it would be an insult to common sense, and a very parody on the Scriptures, to assert that the propitiation is the actual deliverance of all men from the curse of the Law. But this is only a caricature of the doctrine of the universal atonement. The propitiation in itself, apart from its application by the Holy Spirit, and its coincident reception by faith, delivered no man – none even of the elect – from amenability to punishment.* It is an expedient, in consideration of which any man and every man may, and all believers do, obtain this deliverance. On the ground of this atonement, the most unrighteous of men may by faith in it be treated by God as if he were as righteous as Jesus Himself (2 Cor. 5:21). He *may* be delivered from the penal

---

* 'Paul teacheth us, that we be not only justifiable, but justified by Christ's, blood (Rom. 5:9), yet not simply as offered on the cross, but through faith in His blood (Rom. 3:25), that is, through His blood applied by faith.' Ussher's *Judgment*, p. 33. See Note A.

consequences of his transgressions, and judicially acquitted by the just and the justifying God of the gospel; but no man can be actually acquitted – in reality delivered, until by faith he be 'found' in Him in whom God 'hath not beheld iniquity in Jacob, neither hath He seen perverseness in Israel' (Num. 23:21). The blessed propitiation is only THE GROUND OF JUSTIFICATION.

CHAPTER THREE

THE ATONEMENT NOT REDEMPTION

IT IS REMARKABLE how very generally the atonement and redemption are confounded together. It seems to be all but universally taken for granted that they are strictly, but one and the same thing. It appears, moreover, to be pretty evident, that it is from this identification of two very different things that some of the current objections to the universality of the atonement are derived. Men cannot think that Christ has redeemed all sinners; and therefore they cannot be persuaded that He has atoned for all sins.

It is true that Christ has not redeemed all sinners. Redemption is particular, not general. It is to be measured by election, not by the atonement. Christ redeems believers only; and yet He has atoned 'for the sins of the whole world.' Redemption is as distinct from the atonement as the clouds of heaven are from the ocean, up from which they rise. As the clouds are derived from the ocean: so is redemption from the atonement. We might as rationally confound the propitiation with sanctification, as confound it, as some do, with redemption. The propitiation is that incommensurable boon in consideration of which redemption (like sanctification) is obtained by some, and may be obtained by all. Redemption did not take place at Christ's death. It is a blessing that has no existence till the sinner becomes a believer.

Redemption properly means *deliverance* obtained by the payment of a price; it often means deliverance obtained in any manner; it always means actual deliverance.

SECT. 1. That redemption means actual deliverance is evident from many passages of Scripture. For example, Job says, 'Did I say *deliver* me from the enemy's hand? or *redeem* me from the hand of the mighty?' (Job 6:23). The Lord, in Jeremiah, says, 'I will *deliver* thee out of the hand of the wicked, and I will *redeem* thee out of the hand of the terrible' (Jer. 15:21). In Micah it is said, 'There shalt thou be *delivered;* there the Lord shall *redeem* thee from the hand of thine enemies' (Mic. 4:10). There are equally convincing, passages in the New Testament. Take, for example, Luke 21:28, 'And when these things begin to come to pass, then look up, and lift up your heads; for your *redemption* draweth nigh.' Here the term can mean nothing but actual deliverance.[*] And no other meaning can possibly fit that other passage, Romans 8:23, where those who have received 'the first fruits of the Spirit,' are represented as 'groaning within themselves, waiting for the adoption, the *redemption* of their body'; that is, the deliverance of their body from death and corruption, when it 'shall be fashioned like unto the glorious body of the Son of God' (Phil. 3:21). A similar passage occurs in Ephesians 1:14, where it is said of the Spirit, that He is 'the earnest of our inheritance, until the *redemption* of the purchased possession, unto the praise of His glory.' And again, in 5:30, the apostle warns thus, 'Grieve not the Holy Spirit of God, whereby ye are sealed unto the day of *redemption*,' that is, unto the day when all believers – as the acquired and peculiar possession of Jesus (see Acts 20:28) – shall be completely delivered

---

[*] Dr. Campbell justly translates the expression, 'because your *deliverance* approacheth.' – (Gospels.)

from the penal consequences of sin. One other passage may be specified: it is found in Hebrews 11:35, where it is said, 'Women received their dead raised to life again; and others were tortured, not accepting *deliverance,* that they might obtain a better resurrection.' Here the same word that in the other passages is translated redemption, is most appropriately rendered *deliverance,* because the passage is certainly capable of no other meaning. We see clearly, then, from these passages of Scripture, that the proper meaning of the term redemption, is deliverance; and consequently no man can be said to be redeemed, who is not actually delivered.

SECT. 2. The spiritual redemption, which believers receive from Christ, is a twofold deliverance. It is firstly and principally, deliverance from the penalty of the Law; it is secondly and consequently, deliverance from the power of sin. It will not be difficult to show that these two great blessings include the entirety of the spiritual redemption which believers receive from Jesus, or to demonstrate that neither the one deliverance nor the other took place on Calvary, but that both occur when the faith of the individual takes place.

SECT. 3. In the first place, then, it is to be proved that redemption is actual deliverance from the penalty of the Law; and that this actual deliverance is not a reality at all, until the sinner becomes a believer. The first part of this proposition is easily demonstrated. In Ephesians 1:7, we find it is said of God that He hath made believers accepted in the Beloved, in Whom they 'have redemption through His blood, *the forgiveness of sins,* according to the riches of His grace.' A similar statement occurs in Colossians 1:14, where believers are described as being 'translated into the kingdom of God's dear Son, in whom they have redemption through His blood, *the forgiveness of sins.*' Now as these passages are, as it were, an inspired dictionary, in which we have the formal explanation of the term, it is manifest that redemption is a blessing similar to the forgiveness of sins. Robert Haldane, a limitarian 'after the most straitest sect,' very justly says, 'The same thing that is *redemption* is, in another point of view, *forgiveness.*'[*]
Forgiveness of sins and redemption are, then, one and the same blessing, viewed in different aspects. Compare Revelation 5:9, with Colossians 3:13. What then is 'the

---

[*] See his Commentary on Rom. 3:24.

forgiveness of sins'? It is deliverance from the penal consequences of sin. But surely there is no man who will affirm that the believer's sins are remitted or pardoned before they are committed, and ages even before he is born. It is an error, as we have in a former section largely shown, to suppose that remission of sins – in other words that pardon – took place on Calvary. It must, then, be the same error, in another dress, to suppose that redemption took place there and then. How could the elect unborn be actually delivered before they were actually inthralled; nay, before they were actually in being, and thus capable of thraldom or deliverance?

SECT. 4. That redemption did not actually take place on Calvary will be rendered evident from another passage of Scripture. In 1 Corinthians 1:30, it is said of believers that they are 'in Christ Jesus, who of God is made unto them wisdom, and righteousness, and sanctification, and *redemption*.' The meaning of this passage is, that through Christ believers become wise, justified, sanctified, *redeemed*. The question then is, when are they redeemed? The answer is at hand: it is not, at all events, ages before they are 'justified and sanctified.' The apostle, in his chain of blessings, puts redemption *after* justification and sanctification. Not that we are to suppose that there are long intervals between the believer's wisdom, justification, sanctification, and redemption. The four blessings are a single cluster; and the meaning of the apostle is, that whenever a sinner becomes 'wise unto salvation,' through the knowledge of the truth as it is in Jesus, that same moment he is held as righteous; as soon as he is 'righteous by faith' (Rom. 1:17) he begins to be sanctified 'in soul, body, and spirit,' and from that moment he is actually redeemed, or delivered from the penal consequences of his sins (see Rom. 5:10). Christ, then, is 'redemption' to us, in the same sense that He is 'wisdom, and righteousness, and sanctification'; and we should be as much warranted to affirm that Christ on Calvary enlightened the elect, or justified the elect, or sanctified the elect, as we are to say that He there and then redeemed the elect.

SECT. 5. It is indeed a glorious truth, that He there and then 'obtained for us eternal redemption' (Heb. 9:12) just as He there and then 'brought in everlasting righteousness' for us (Dan. 9:24). It is a glorious truth, that ever since the work given Him to do was 'finished,' there is 'plenteous redemption' 'IN

Him'[*] (Rom. 3:24) just as there is plenteous salvation 'IN HIM' (2 Tim. 2:10) and plenty and to spare of 'eternal life' 'IN HIM' (1 Jn 5:11; Jn 5:26). But it would be a most unwarrantable abuse of language, and a strange perversion of those simple and delightful truths, were any man to conclude that Christ, upon the cross, actually made righteous, and saved, and redeemed, and vivified those who were yet unbelievers and unborn.

SECT. 6. But perhaps someone might be disposed to say, 'Is it not, however, expressly said, that "Christ *redeemed* believers from the curse of the law, being made a curse for them?"' (Gal. 3:13, see also Gal. 4:5). And are not believers represented as saying, 'Thou wast slain, and *hast redeemed* us to God by thy blood'? (Rev. 5:9). Is it not plain from these passages that believers were redeemed at the time that Christ 'was slain,' and 'became a curse for them'? Yes, indeed, it is true that all believers are redeemed; but it is no more evident from these passages that they were redeemed 1,800 years ago than it is evident from 1 Peter 1:18, that they were then redeemed (that is, delivered) from the dominion of inherent corruption. It is there

---

[*] See Note B

The Atonement Not Redemption

said that believers 'were redeemed with the precious blood of Jesus, from their vain conversation.' Christ is said to 'have washed believers from their sins in His blood' (Rev. 1:5) but it would surely be a misinterpretation were any person to gather from this passage that they were actually washed before they were 'unclean' (see Psa. 51:7).[*] Christ hath 'delivered believers from the wrath to come' (1 Thess. 1:10); but we know that none are delivered until they become believers (Rom. 7:5, 6; see also Eph. 2:3). God 'hath quickened believers together with Christ' (Eph. 2:5); but we know that they are not quickened before they have faith (Eph. 2:8); nay, they are not, they cannot be quickened before they be 'dead in trespasses and sins' (Eph. 2:1). Whenever sinners become believers, then they are 'quickened,' 'saved,' 'delivered,' 'washed'; and it is then, also, AND THEN ONLY, that they are 'redeemed' from the penalty of the Law. Whilst Christ, then, on the cross atoned for all sins, past, present, and future, it is not true that He there and

---

[*] "'The blood of Christ,' saith St. John (1 Jn 1:7), 'cleanseth us from all sin'; yet cleanse it doth not by being prepared, but by being applied. Prepared it was, when He poured it out once upon the cross; applied it is, when He washeth us from our sins therein (Rev. 1: 5). Usher's *Judgment of the Extent of Christ's Death*, p. 33.

then redeemed all. But He there and then laid down the price of redemption, on the ground of which any and all shall be redeemed or delivered, if they but believe God's record regarding Him.

SECT. 7. The other part of the spiritual redemption which believers obtain from Christ, is deliverance from the power of sin. It would be idle to spend time in proving that this deliverance did not actually take place upon the cross. Deliverance from the power of sin is but another name for sanctification; and though it be a glorious truth that provision was there and then made for the holiness of all believers, it is surely not a truth at all that they were there and then made holy. This holiness is, however, a necessary and integrant part of the redemption of Jesus. Christ 'gave Himself for us,' said an apostle to believers, 'that He might redeem us from all iniquity, and purify [us] to Himself a peculiar people, zealous of good works' (Tit. 2:14); and believers are reminded by another apostle in a passage already referred to, 'that they were redeemed, not with corruptible things as silver and gold, from their vain conversation, received by tradition from their fathers; but with the precious blood of Christ, as of a lamb without blemish and without spot' (1 Pet.

1:18–19). If all who are redeemed by Christ are, according to the spirit of these passages, actually sanctified, it is quite clear that instead of being really redeemed by Christ on Calvary, there was there and then made only the preparation of provision for their ultimate deliverance. Christ, at His death, 'obtained' for them 'eternal redemption' (Heb. 9:12).

SECT. 8. It will be seen then, how great is the difference between redemption and the propitiation. Universal redemption is but another name for universal salvation and universal santification. Of such a universalism, surely no student of the Bible could for a moment dream. It would give the lie to apostles and prophets, to common sense and common facts. No wonder that many earnest students have a horror of the sound of universal propitiation, seeing they have not been taught to distinguish between the propitiation and redemption. They have supposed that they were but different names of identically the same thing. But this is no more true than that the propitiation and sanctification are one and the same thing. Believers only are sanctified, and they are sanctified only after they become believers. Believers only are redeemed, and they are redeemed only after they become believers.

Their sins, however, were atoned for 1,800 years ago. The propitiation, then, is THE BASIS, THE GROUND of redemption. It is THE PRICE OF REDEMPTION. It is THE RANSOM for all. It is *that* in consideration of which the most 'high-handed' sinner on earth may for ever, as to state, be delivered from the punishment of his crimes; and may now, as to his character, be delivered from the tyranny of corruption. How glorious the truth there *is* 'plenteous redemption' for all. There is 'enough and to spare' in an infinite atonement for all. Do not, O do not suppose, 'heavy-laden' sinner, that any peculiar favourites may have been delivered from the burden of their guilt on Calvary, but perhaps not you. Nothing exclusive of you was then accomplished. None were then redeemed, but a meritorious cause was then effected, on the ground of which you and all others may enjoy the blessings of complete redemption.[*] Glory be to God!

---

[*] Dr. Payne accurately distinguished redemption from the atonement. *Lectures, p.* 222 – 'Redemption is the effect of the atonement. It is the actual deliverance of its subject from condemnation, sin, and misery, on the ground of the atonement, or the price of redemption paid by the Son of God. Redemption therefore must be particular, or we must admit the unscriptural doctrine of universal salvation.'

Chapter Four

The Atonement Not Reconciliation

Unhappily the propitiation has often been confounded with reconciliation. This may have arisen partly from the primary meaning of the word atonement. Its obvious composition is at-one-ment. It has reference to parties, who, having been alienated, are again brought to be AT ONE. When a onement is effected between such parties there is reconciliation. The word atonement occurs in this sense in the old English writers. Shakespeare, for example, says '— he seeks to make *atonement* / Between the Duke of Glo'ster and your brothers.'

There the term evidently means reconciliation. In the fine old version of the New Testament by Tyndale, that passage in

2 Corinthians 5:19, which is properly translated in our version, 'and hath committed unto us the word of reconciliation,' is rendered 'and hath committed unto us the preaching of the atonement.' In the only passage of the New Testament where the word atonement occurs, it is evidently to be understood in this old sense of at-one-ment. The passage is found in Romans 5:11, 'We also joy in God, through our Lord Jesus Christ, by whom we have now received the atonement.' The word here rendered atonement is the same that, in 2 Corinthians 5:19, is translated reconciliation; and the meaning of the whole expression obviously is, 'by whom we have received the reconciliation'; that is, 'by whom we have been reconciled.'[*] It has exclusive reference to the reconciliation which takes place in the sinner's heart when he becomes a believer. The verb, of which the word in question is the noun, is translated 'reconciled' in the preceding verse. We cannot then learn what the atonement is from this passage of the New Testament, for here the word has the antiquated and obsolete sense in which it is not now used,

---

[*] 'To receive reconciliation, and to be reconciled, are, of course, synonymous expressions' – Hodge on the passage.

and refers exclusively to what takes place in the heart of the believer. At-one-ment, or reconciliation on man's part, is one of the blessings derived from the atonement; but it is not the atonement itself.

SECT. 1. There are obviously three, and only three, senses in which the atonement could be said to be reconciliation. It might be meant, first, that it had actually brought to be at one, God and man. In this case the reconciliation is regarded as reciprocal, having reference to both the parties. It might be meant, secondly, that the atonement did actually reconcile man to God. In this case the reconciliation is all on man's part. It might be meant, thirdly, that the atonement. actually reconciled God to man. In this case the reconciliation is all on God's part. As to the first of these opinions, none, but such as dream of a universal salvation, could for a moment entertain it. As to the second, it is true that the atonement is the means whereby man *may* be reconciled to God; but, as this reconciliation on man's part is but another name for sanctification, no accurate-minded man could for a moment confound it with the atonement, which is certainly not actual sanctification (or at-one-ment with God), but only the moral medium by which it may be obtained. It is, then, only in reference to the third opinion that there is any dispute. Is it true that the atonement is the reconciliation of God either to the elect, or to all men? This is the question. If it be true that it was at the death of Christ that God was reconciled, and if His reconciliation were then limited within the boundaries of the elect then there can be no hope that those without these boundaries can ever get God to be their friend, except by a second atonement. The non-elect's case would be utterly hopeless and helpless. If, on the other hand, God be actually, by the death of Christ, already reconciled to the world, or to all men, irrespective of their 'submission to His righteousness,' then some may very naturally be inclined to wonder why any of the human race should ever experience the 'vengeance' of His 'indignation.' It would seem to be wrong to say, either on the limited or the unlimited scheme, that God was reconciled by the death of Christ. We cannot conceive the propitiation to be reconciliation on God's part in any legitimate sense whatsoever.

SECT. 2. Some of those who conceive the propitiation either to be, or by itself to have effected, the reconciliation of God to man, speak of God's 'enmity to our rebellious race'; and it is this 'enmity,' which they conceive (in the case of the elect at least) to have been removed by the atonement.[*] The truth, however, appears to be that, though man's heart is 'enmity against God' (Rom. 8:7), God's heart was never enmity against man. 'GOD IS LOVE'. This, His name, is also His nature. His very justice as a moral governor, as Stillingfleet with axiomatic accuracy remarks, is 'but His goodness directed by wisdom.' God is not even the enemy of devils. As a judge, He must condemn them; but as the Father of their being, He feels for them. Even an earthly judge may, as a private individual, greatly love and pity the criminal against whom he is compelled to denounce the severe sentence of the law. So far from God being man's enemy, He has ever been man's friend. The atonement did not purchase, as with a bribe, God's kindness, and make Him our friend; it is an effect and proof of His friendliness, it is the fruit of His 'unspeakable love' and 'philanthropy' (see Tit. 3:4, 'man-love'). Pomponius Atticus, the amiable and accomplished friend of Cicero, in a funeral oration which he pronounced on the death of his mother, asserted that 'though he had resided with her for sixty-seven years, yet he

---

[*] As, for example, R. Haldane (*Com. on* Rom. v. 10).

was never reconciled to her.'[*] The reason was, there had never been the least discord between them. *We*, indeed, have discorded with God; 'by wicked works' we have made ourselves His 'enemies,' and consequently *we* require to be reconciled to Him. He, however, never ceased to be our friend, and consequently *He* never required to be reconciled. In Scripture it is man alone, and never God, who is said to be reconciled.[†] Hence the apostle Paul, being himself 'reconciled to God by Jesus Christ,' received from Him 'the ministry of reconciliation,' and, as an 'ambassador for Christ,' prayed men, as though OUR FRIEND GOD HIMSELF 'did beseech' them by him, '*be ye reconciled unto God.*' 'God was in Christ reconciling the

---

[*] Cornelii Nepotis vitæ, cap. xvii. Cornelius Nepos was the intimate friend of Atticus.

[†] See, on this subject, a valuable dissertation by that uncommonly clear-headed man, R. Riccaltoun of Hobkirk. It is contained in pp. 373–390 of the first volume of his Works. Moses Stuart, of Andover, says (*Com. on Rom.* v. 10), 'The scriptural view of reconciliation is that the offending party becomes reconciled to the other.' Some persons may be remembering Ezekiel 16:63, 'When I am pacified toward thee for all that thou hast done.' Sometimes this passage is referred to as proof that God is said to be reconciled. The proof, however, depends on a mistranslation, as must be evident to every Hebrew scholar. The passage should have been rendered thus, 'Because I have forgiven to thee all that thou hast done. (*See* Dathe.) It is thus that the same word is translated, Psalm 78:38; Jeremiah 18:23, etc.

world unto Himself' (2 Cor. 5:18–20). It is not said or meant, that He was 'reconciling Himself unto the world.' When it is said by the apostle (Rom. 11:15) that 'the casting away of the Jews was the reconciling of the world' (that is, of the Gentiles), we are not to understand him as intimating that the rejection of the former was the means of reconciling God to the latter. He means that that dispensation toward the Jews was graciously overruled in such a manner as to become the means by which the Gentile world might be reconciled to God. Ancient believers, 'when they were enemies,' are said (Rom. 5:10) 'to have been reconciled to God by the death of His Son'; by which we are surely to understand the slaying of the enmity of their hearts, by the knowledge and belief of God's love manifested in Christ's death. They are 'reconciled by Christ's death' in the same sense that they are 'justified by His blood' (Rom. 5:9), *viz.*, only after they become believers.* Until then they are all

---

* 'That which is said in Romans 5:10, 'when we were enemies we were reconciled to God by the death of His Son,' has no other meaning than this, – men are transformed from a state of enmity into a state of actual reconciliation with God, through the death of Christ, as soon as they believe on Christ.' – Davenant *(de Morte Christi).*

declared to be 'enemies of God' (Rom. 5:10; Col. 1:21).

SECT. 3. We are perfectly aware that some of these expressions to which we have referred, have been supposed by certain writers to convey a meaning quite opposite to that which we have adopted, and which they naturally suggest. They have sometimes been interpreted as if they denoted the reconciliation of God to man, instead of the reconciliation of man to God. In support of this explication, appeal has been made to that passage of our Lord's sermon on the Mount, 'First be reconciled to thy brother, and then come and offer thy gift.' 'This passage,' says Dr. Symington, 'is most decisive. The person addressed is the offender: he has nothing against his brother, but his brother hath something against him; yet he is exhorted to go and be reconciled to his brother, that is to go and reconcile his brother to himself. This is the only meaning which the passage can bear, consistently with the terms employed. On the same principle, when man is required to be reconciled to God, may we not be warranted to conclude that the phrase implies that God is to be reconciled to man?"[*] We say no; and we say so for three reasons: 1. This supposition would make God even yet to be unreconciled; for we are beseeched to be *now* reconciled unto God. Even on this hypothesis therefore God could not be said to be reconciled at and by the death of Christ. 2. The supposition would imply that it is sinners themselves that are to reconcile God. If the expression in our Saviour's sermon, 'be reconciled to thy brother,' means, 'reconcile thy brother to thyself,' then the expression in Paul's epistle, 'be ye reconciled to God,' must mean, 'reconcile God unto yourselves'; but who will dare to say that it must or *may* mean that? 3. The passage in Matthew, on which the interpretation is built, establishes quite the opposite hypothesis. It is true, that the person who is commanded to leave his gift was the offender, and he alone; but on this very account, he was the enemy; it was he, and he alone, that had manifested a spirit of enmity; and what he is commanded to do, is to lay aside his enmity toward his brother. It is possible that his brother, though the

---

[*] 'On the Atonement,' p. 26. Dr. Symington would by no means speak of God's enmity, though, along with many other writers, he explains as above, the passages referred to. See also Dr. Wardlaw's 'Nature and Extent of the Atonement,' pp. 31–32.

injured party, might never have become his enemy in return; and if he had, it is still possible that his enmity could not by any means be propitiated. What the offender was required to do, was not to avert his brother's enmity, but to remove the cause of offence, by himself ceasing to manifest the part of an enemy, and by showing without delay his penitence, and friendliness, and love. In our relation to God, it is man and man alone, that is the offender; man, and man alone, is the enemy; and therefore man, and man alone, has enmity to lay aside; and man, and man alone, is in a capacity to be reconciled. It is quite wrong therefore, and, as it appears to us, very dishonouring to the tender mercies and loving-kindness of God, to speak of His enmity against man being removed by the death of Christ.

SECT. 4. Some excellent theologians, however, are in the habit of using the expression, that God has, by the cross, been reconciled to the world,[*] in the sense, that is, of His judicial anger being then averted. There is certainly a great difference between anger and enmity. A kind king may be judicially angry, very angry, at some disobedient subjects, and this anger may lead

---

[*] As, for example, Dr. Payne, *Lectures*, pp. 140–142.

him to punish them severely; but it would be false to say that he was their enemy. God, though 'Love,' can be angry. And 'when His wrath is kindled but a little,' well may the stoutest heart begin to quake. What, O what must be His 'hot displeasure' in 'the day of wrath and revelation of the righteous judgement of God' (Rom. 2:4). God's anger is of course no passion; there is no malignity, no vindictiveness in it. It is a principle, and a principle, moreover, that has existence only in reference to His rectoral relation. But the anger of God was not averted by the death of Christ, apart from the sinner's personal faith in that death. So far from it being then averted, 'God is angry with the wicked every day.' Believers themselves were 'by nature the children of wrath, even as others' (Eph. 2:3). The wrath of God was 'on them,' till they believed (see Jn 3:36; Rom. 4:15; 1 Thess. 1:10). It is true, true, true indeed, that on the cross such a satisfaction was made to God on our behalf as sinners – such a display of His hatred of our sin, and His regard to His Law, that now He is no longer, required, in justice to punish our transgressions. A something was then effected in consideration of which that judicial displeasure, which consists in His determination to punish the sinner, may be averted, and averted most honourably to himself, and most safely to His empire. This is true, indeed, and most cheering truth; but it is not true that His anger is actually 'turned away,' until we actually turn away from our sins (Isa. 12:1).

SECT. 5. Is it said by any, 'O, but it was predicted that Christ was to "make reconciliation for iniquity" (Dan. 9:24); and it is expressly asserted by the apostle, that "He made reconciliation for the sins of the people" (Heb. 2:17). Do not these passages seem to intimate that there really was reconciliation on God's part effected by the cross?' They only seem so to an English reader. In both places, as is evident to any person who has even only dipped into the original languages, the word 'propitiation' should have been employed instead of the word 'reconciliation'. None of the original words have any relation to the term which in 2 Corinthians 5:18, is acknowledged by all parties to be accurately rendered 'reconciliation'. But some may be inclined still to object, and say, 'Is not the apostle's mode of expression in 2 Corinthians 5:19, "God *was* in Christ reconciling the world unto Himself," indicative of reconciliation that actually took place at the death of Christ?' No; 'God was in Christ reconciling the world unto Himself,' only in the sense of

The Atonement Not Reconciliation

then doing a *something*, the moral influence of which is adapted to reconcile sinners to Himself, by slaying the enmity of their hearts (see Eph. 2:16); *which something* was also a sufficient ground on which He might consistently turn Himself from His judicial determination to punish sin, whenever any sinner should by faith betake himself unto the 'city of refuge.'

SECT. 6. We, therefore, make appeal to the unbelieving sinner, not to suppose that God is reconciled in the sense of not being displeased and angry. He is angry. True, He is not your foe; O no! 'He so loved you,' as to give the Son of His bosom to die for you. How could a foe be such a Friend? And how cruel is it in you to requite such love with such indifference, nay, with such hatred! O shame! Shame to you. Is it not, moreover, cruel to yourself to provoke the unutterable judicial wrath of such unutterable 'love'? O why will you cause God to have recourse to His 'strange act'? O why will you compel love itself to become anger to you? We beseech you to be NOW reconciled unto God. That which is required of you is that you believe that God is your Friend; believe that He loves *you;* believe that in token of this, He gave His Son to be a propitiation for your sins. O be persuaded to believe that GOD IS ALREADY

YOUR FRIEND, and that He is only waiting for you, in 'this the day of salvation,' to reciprocate the affection, that then His anger may be turned away for ever. The atonement is not reconciliation: IT IS A SOMETHING BY MEANS OF WHICH BELIEVERS ARE, AND ALL MEN MAY BE, RECONCILED TO GOD.

CHAPTER FIVE

THE ATONEMENT NOT PAYMENT OF DEBT

PERHAPS THIS STATEMENT may be apt to startle you. The opinion opposed may possibly be one which you may be said to have sucked in with your mother's milk. It is a favourite idea, nay, an axiom with some theologians, that Christ, at His death, and by His death, fully liquidated the whole debt of sin which the elect have contracted. They look upon the work of Calvary as a sort of pecuniary transaction, in which Christ, as the accepted Surety of believers, gave to the Father so much punishment for so many sins.* They conceive the sinner to be owing God a certain amount of penalty, which was then all paid and cleared. In a little tract, published by the London Tract Society, and entitled 'Good News,' there occurs the following paragraph, which may be regarded as representative of millions more. 'Suppose a spendthrift who had wasted his money in riotous living had contracted many debts which he was utterly unable to pay should hear that some great benefactor on whom he had no claim whatever had unexpectedly discharged all his debts, would he not welcome the good news with the deepest gratitude? Such, reader, are the glad tidings, and infinitely more precious, which I would bring you this day.' Here it is taken for granted that the debt of the sinner is already actually 'discharged' by the death of Christ; and that this is really the case, with respect to the elect at least, we suppose there are thousands who never entertained a moment's doubt. From the strain in which many persons talk and others write, one might be led to anticipate that every page of

---

* In one passage of the New Testament Christ is called 'a surety' (Heb. 7:22); but he would be an extraordinary expositor who could find in the expression there, any allusion to debt-paying. The Greek Fathers, who knew their own language best, all explain the phrase by Hebrews 8:6.

the Bible must be speaking of the payment of the sinner's debt; whereas, it is a remarkable fact, that there is not a single hint or allusion to such a pecuniary transaction from Genesis to Revelation. The great atonement is never represented in Scripture as the payment of a debt. If accompanied with great limitations and modifications, the simile may be allowed as an occasional illustration of the great moral transaction of Calvary; but it is quite extra-scriptural in its origin, and to regard it as an adequate, and as some seem to do, even a consecrated, key to unlock the mysteries of the cross, is to put man's device in the place of God's 'witty invention.' There are some weighty considerations which induce us so strongly to assert that the atonement is not the payment of a debt.

SECT. 1. *Debts when paid cease to be debts; but sin, though atoned for, is a debt still.* If you had been formerly in debt to any man, and had long ago got all paid, either by your own exertions or by a representative, you could not be said to be in debt still. No man, with justice or propriety, could call you a debtor. Your debt is obliterated – it has no existence. If, then, Christ, by His death, actually paid the debt of the elect, the elect are no longer debtors, and their sins can no longer with justice or propriety be denominated 'debts.'

It is a fact, however, that their sins are 'debts' still; for the Saviour Himself has taught them, in His own epitome of prayer, to use, and daily too, this petition, 'Forgive us our debts, as we forgive our debtors' (Matt. 6:12). The atonement, then, must undoubtedly be something else than the payment of these debts.

SECT. 2. *Debts which are paid cannot be forgiven; but though sin is atoned for, it must also be forgiven.* If some person who had been owing you a hundred pounds, which you were determined to exact, should obtain the sum from a generous friend, and pay you to the 'uttermost farthing' would it not be an insult at once to justice and to common sense were you to go away and talk of your kindness in forgiving him his debt? Why, the debt was paid; and being paid, it could not possibly be forgiven, unless you returned him the money you received. Now, if the atonement of Christ be like the payment of a debt, it would be a flagrant inconsistency to say that the debt has been forgiven; and it would be a strange anomaly were the discharged debtor to go and beg the pardon of his liquidated debts. The sinner is, however, commanded to pray humbly and earnestly every day that his 'debts may be forgiven'; and we therefore conclude that whatever the atonement may be, it was not the payment and discharge of these 'debts.'

SECT. 3. *Debts may be forgiven without any payment; but sin could not be forgiven without an atonement.* If any person owes you a sum of money, you are not obliged to exact it. You may generously and mercifully remit it. If, then, our sins were merely 'debts,' (and not CRIMES) God, as our great creditor, would be under no necessity to exact payment. It would be quite consistent with His sovereign character, like 'the Lord of the servant' in the parable, to be 'moved with compassion, and loose us, and forgive us our debts' (Matt. 18:27). One would naturally expect, indeed, seeing His name is 'Love,' that 'when we had nothing to pay, He would frankly forgive us' (Lk. 7:42). But sin is something more than a debt, and God is something more than our creditor. Sin is a crime, and God is the universal Governor; and without an atonement, sin could not be pardoned. 'Without shedding of blood there is no remission; it was therefore necessary' (Heb. 9:22–23), and 'of necessity' (Heb. 8:3), that Jesus, as our atoning priest, 'should have somewhat to offer.' It became God to exact such a sacrifice, and Jesus 'ought to have suffered those things' (Heb. 2:10; Luke 24:26). The atonement, then, must have been something widely different from the mere payment of a debt.

SECT. 4. *Debts are transferable, sins are not.* If any friend of yours contracts a debt, you may become responsible for it, and then he is no longer himself responsible to the creditor. If you, moreover, having once transferred upon yourself the responsibility for the debt should pay the whole, he could no longer be liable for the consequences of his debt. He is no longer a debtor; neither could he lawfully be subjected to any pains and penalties, although he neither has nor could have paid one fraction of his debt. The debt was in whole transferred to you; you were voluntarily liable to all the consequences of the debt, and, upon failure of payment, it is you who would have been subjected to all the penal consequences. It is quite otherwise with sin. It is not transferable. If another commit a theft, the sin could not be transferred to you or to Christ, so that you or He should be the thief. The effects of sin are transferable, but not sin itself. Jesus could never have become the debtor – the sinner. He could never have deserved to suffer the consequences of sin; neither could he ever so suffer the consequences as to liberate us from deserving punishment. The believer does not obtain deliverance as a right; he implores it as a favour (Lk. 18:13). The imprisoned debtor, as soon as he has obtained an able friend to pay his debt, may demand his immediate release; he can no longer deserve to suffer punishment. The reason is, he is no longer a debtor, because his debt is paid. The sinner is, however, still a sinner, though his sins are atoned for. His sins cannot be so transferred to Christ that they cease to be his own. He has still to implore forgiveness; aye, and it is mercy manifold if God do not 'hold him guilty'. Hence it is clear that the propitiation cannot have been the mere payment of a debt.

SECT. 5. *The satisfactory payment of a debt does not depend on the dignity of the person who pays it; but the whole value of the propitiation depends upon the high and glorious rank and character of the Sufferer.* The first part of the proposition requires no illustration. If some poor man were owing you £100, and if he were getting a great nobleman to become responsible for his debt, you would not take £10 from the nobleman as this, though given by 'never so great' a personage, is an adequate discharge of the debt. It is far otherwise, however, with the propitiation. Its value does not depend upon the amount of suffering endured, but chiefly on the majesty of the God-man who suffered.* A mere man could undoubtedly have been so sustained by the omnipotence of God, as to have endured as great an amount of suffering as was borne by Jehovah-Jesus. It was the humanity alone of the Son of God which did or could suffer. Divinity could not possibly be pained. The 'sword awoke against the man, Jehovah's fellow' Zech. 13:7. 'A *body* did God prepare Him' (Heb. 10:5), that 'through the offering of *the body* (that is, the human nature) of Jesus Christ' (Heb. 10:10), 'we might be sanctified.' It was His 'soul 'that was 'made an offering for sin' (Isa. 53:10), and it was in His body that He bore our sins on the tree (1 Pet. 2:24). Now, if Divinity is impassible, and if it was His human nature alone that obeyed and suffered, is it not plain that He, as God, could have sustained the human nature of some spotless creature under an equal load of agonies? That man's idea of the propitiation is *low*, who places its value in the amount of pain endured, either in body or in soul. The value of the propitiation must be entirely attributed to the ineffable glory of the 'God in man,' Who,

---

* Hence the principal, or rather the whole importance of the controversy regarding the proper divinity of the Saviour. The whole value of the atonement rests and hinges on Christ's Deity.

by His obedience to the precept and endurance of the penalty, 'magnified the law, and made it honourable.' The value of a payment, however, never in any case can depend upon the character or rank of the person who pays, but solely upon the amount paid. Now it is clearly demonstrable that Jesus Himself could not possibly have paid the full amount and degree of punishment to which even *any one sinner* is liable. A seared conscience and a hardened heart are evidently principal and most fearful ingredients in the woes of the condemned; but such a conscience and such a heart could never have a place within the bosom of the spotless Lamb of God. Christ did not, then, in the glorious atonement, pay the exact amount of suffering which the sinner had incurred. The glory and lustre of His character – being the uncreated and creating God, Who, as God, made the Law, and, as God, could not be subject to the Law – more than swelled out the deficit in the amount of penalty endured, to an infinitude of value. His obedience to the precept, and His endurance of the penalty of the insulted Law, did more to demonstrate God's regard to its excellence, His determination to punish its transgression, and His abhorrence of any violation of its precepts, than could have been manifested in the final and eternal perdition of the whole human race. No being can say or think *now*, though God pardons many sins, forgives without payment many debts, that He is not a sin-hating God.

SECT. 6. How different then the whole transaction from a commercial bargain! How degrading to regard God, Who is uniformly in Scripture represented as 'FORGIVING our debts,' in the attitude of a 'creditor severe,' demanding relentlessly the full payment of His dues. How rash is it in man, with his little puny paltry ingenuity, to devise and consecrate a far-fetched, inadequate and unnatural simile by which to cramp, crib, quadrate, and pervert the majestically unique, sublimely great, and infinitely generous and glorious transaction of the cross! Instead of this, let us stretch out our minds to grasp at the true nature of the propitiation; and let us never invert the process, and attempt to clip it, and fit it, and terrestrialize it down to our minds. It is not because Jesus bore so many stripes for so many sins that we can venture our soul upon His merit. It is because the Bible tells us, that Jesus as the Son of God, through His own eternal Spirit',[*] made Himself a sacrifice, made His soul an offering for us, that without alarm, or one quiver of fear, we can risk on Him our whole interests, and lay on Him our whole burden, howsoever great. Nay, though we had accumulated on ourselves all the iniquities of all the monsters of humanity that ever wallowed in the mire of sin, seeing it is 'Immanuel' that is the 'propitiation,' we should be without fear. The debt of our sin never was paid, never (if we perish not) will or can be paid. We trust that instead of being *exacted*, it will be freely, fully, frankly, and for ever *forgiven;* and the propitiation of Jesus we regard as a glorious *something,* which certainly does not make payment of our debts, but in consideration of which they may without payment be pardoned. SIN WAS ATONED FOR AS A CRIME NOT AS A DEBT. To suppose the propitiation to be the payment of our sin-debts, is, in another aspect, to confound the propitiation and pardon.

SECT. 7. It appears to us that multitudes, indeed that whole swarms, of the objections that are commonly made to the unlimited extent of the propitiation, owe their birth to

---

[*] That this expression (Heb. ix. 14) refers to the Divine nature of Christ is now admitted by almost all competent expositors

this mercantile idea of the work of Christ. It is thought, and justly too, that it would be unjust in God to exact double payment of the same debts – once from the Surety, and again, and for ever, from the finally impenitent. It is thought, and justly too, that it would have been absurd, and even ridiculous in Christ, to have paid a second time the debt of those who were, before His death, already in torments, paying for themselves the penalty of the Law which they had broken. If the propitiation were the payment of a debt, all this would be unanswerable. If Christ would have paid less, had fewer been saved; and more, had none been lost – subtracting or adding so many stripes in consideration of so many sins – all such objections would be logic indeed. But if the propitiation be not at all a transaction bearing even the remotest resemblance to the payment of a debt, or the giving of so much for so many; if it be a glorious device, which only rendered it right in God to forgive any or every debt, without any payment, and which would have been equally required had there been only one sinner to be saved, and only one sin to be pardoned; and by looking forward to which from the dispensation that is past, or looking back to which from the dispensation that is present, any and every sinner may go and crave, and get remission of his debts – if the propitiation be this, every objection to its universality is palsied, every difficulty is paralysed, and it stands forth to *every* sinner seeking salvation, 'majestic in its own simplicity,' as 'the shadow of a great rock in a weary land' (Isa. 32:2).

The propitiation, then, is A SOMETHING, in consideration of which GOD IS READY, INSTEAD OF EXACTING PAYMENT, TO FORGIVE US OUR DEBTS.

Chapter Six

The Atonement: What It Is

WE PROCEED NOW to wind up this treatise by stating what we conceive the propitiation to be. We have already proved that it is not PARDON, but a blessing on the ground of which all sins and sinners *may* be pardoned. It is not DELIVERANCE FROM THE CONDEMNATION OF THE LAW, but a blessing on the ground of which all who have been 'under wrath' may be accepted and treated by God, as if they were righteous with the righteous Jesus Himself. It is not REDEMPTION, but a blessing on the ground of which every miserable captive of Satan *may* for ever be emancipated from his accursed slavery. It is not RECONCILIATION, but a something calculated to slay the bitterest enmity of the wickedest heart.

It is not THE PAYMENT OF A DEBT, but a blessing in consideration of which God *may* now consistently remit unpaid every debt of every sinner. What, then, is THIS WONDERFUL BLESSING? In other words, what is THE PROPITIATION? Our answer is the following:

> *It is an expedient introduced into the Divine moral government, consisting of the obedience unto death of Jesus Christ, which has completely removed all legal obstacles standing between man and the attainability of salvation.*

SECT. 1. The propitiation is a reality, independently of the sinner's faith in it. It is the object on which faith terminates. It is, in this respect, essentially different from pardon, justification, redemption, and reconciliation. The sinner is not called upon to believe that he is pardoned, justified, redeemed, or at one with God. Were he to believe this, he would be believing what is not true till he become a believer. The sinner is, however, called upon to believe that his sins have been atoned for; and consequently this must be something that is true whether he believe it or not. When we assert that

Jesus atoned for sins, we do not mean that He pardoned, justified, redeemed, or reconciled sinners; we mean this, that He removed every *legal* obstacle standing between them and pardon, justification, redemption, and reconciliation; so that if they be not pardoned, justified, redeemed, reconciled, it is their own fault, and they remain for ever 'without excuse.'

SECT. 2. When we say that Jesus removed every *legal* obstacle standing between the sinner and pardon, justification, redemption, and reconciliation, let it be observed that the meaning is not, that He has removed every obstacle of every kind. He has left one obstacle unremoved; but it is one which men are able and called upon to put away. This remaining obstacle, in the case of all gospel hearers, is just their unbelief that all other obstacles are removed. These other obstacles, which were removed by Jesus, were legal obstacles, obstacles arising out of God's relation to us as a righteous Governor. That you may form a clear idea of the nature of these obstacles, consider, for example, the state of the fallen angels. There is no obstacle of unbelief standing between them and salvation, but there is an insuperable *legal* obstacle. Were God, without any propitiation, to save devils, the whole universe of intelligences might begin to say, 'Ah! It is not true that God has an infinite respect for His Law, which He has enjoined upon us, for here we see Him restoring to His favour those who have paid no regard to its requirements. It is not true that He infinitely abhors sin; for here we see that He has ceased to manifest His detestation of it.[*] It is not true that He is determined to put down everything that is calculated to invade the order, harmony, and prosperity of His moral empire; for lo! He has admitted rebels and traitors to the enjoyment of equal happiness with those who have scrupulously regulated their conduct and feelings by the prescribed rule of right. Ah! God is neither just, holy, nor good; or justice, holiness, and goodness are but empty names. Why need we be careful to obey His laws, seeing that they are not respected by Himself?' If such sentiments as these were once to rise up in the minds of God's intelligent creatures, it is manifest that their confidence in Him, and reverence for Him, would immediately be at an end; and if it be true that the creature's holiness and happiness depend entirely on this confidence and reverence, there would, in

---

[*] See some most powerful illustrations of this idea in Dr. West's 'Scripture Doctrine of Atonement.'

the case supposed, soon be nothing but wickedness and woe throughout the immensity of God's universe. But God's love will never permit Him to do anything that would be calculated to undermine the confidence, and diminish the reverence of His intelligent creatures; and seeing that His Law is but the transcript and mirror of His own moral character and glory, it is impossible to conceive that He could ever lay aside His respect for it, by ceasing to maintain its authority, or vindicate its majesty when dishonoured by disobedience. As, then, the fallen angels have dishonoured it by most wilful disobedience, God has been pleased to show His infinite regard for its excellence, and His unutterable detestation of its violation, by visiting upon them the full penalty they have incurred. Thus His conduct toward the angels is such as is calculated to strike awe into the hearts of all His other subjects, and to convince them that impunity in rebellion is a hopeless and reachless chimera. They must surely perceive that hope of happiness is to be found only in the maintenance of holiness. You perceive, then, what an insuperable obstacle stands between devils and salvation. Since there has been no atonement for them, God could not save them without virtually undeifying

Himself in the minds of all those creatures who have intelligence enough to discern, that respect for His own Law is the diadem with which, as the Divine Governor of the universe, He is and must be crowned.

SECT. 3. The nature of the obstacle standing between devils and salvation may perhaps be still more easily apprehended, and still more familiarly explained, by reference to an interesting incident recorded in the life of Daniel. We are informed that, when the spiteful presidents and princes failed to supplant him in the favour of the monarch, they fell upon the serpentine device of getting up an unalterable decree, that no man should offer any petition for thirty days to any God or man, but to King Darius alone. Daniel, of course, chose to disobey man's decree, rather than violate God's command. He continued, three times every day, to present his supplications before the only 'Hearer of prayer.' When his disobedience was reported to Darius, it is said, 'Then the king was sore displeased with himself, and set his heart on Daniel to deliver him; and he laboured till the going down of the sun to deliver him,' and he could not: 'then the king commanded, and they brought Daniel, and cast him into the den of lions' (Dan. 6). Here we see the insuperable obstacle that stood between Daniel and deliverance. Darius loved him: Darius was 'sore displeased with himself' for having issued so foolish a decree; yet Darius was bound over, by the relation in which he stood to his empire and the laws by which it was governed, to inflict upon him the full amount of penalty. Had he, by all his 'labouring to deliver' his favourite, found out some *expedient*, by which respect to his decree, and to his laws in general, could have been as effectually secured as by the personal punishment of the transgressor, Daniel would have got free. As, however, no such expedient could be discovered, it was necessary that Daniel, beloved as he was, should be subjected to the full penalty of the law which he had broken.

SECT. 4. Such was the nature of the obstacle that stood between Daniel and deliverance. Corresponding is the barrier that still intervenes between fallen angels and that pardon, justification, redemption, and reconciliation, which are attainable by fallen men. This barrier has been, in our case, completely and for ever removed. An expedient, a most 'witty invention', has been found out, in consideration of which, God is no longer constrained to visit us with the punishment of our crimes. He can, with perfect honour to His own character, and perfect safety to His government, admit us to His favour. Though God pardon, justify, redeem, reconcile, glorify any one of the human race, no being in the wide universe, can enstamp a stigma against His character, and accuse him of being indifferent to holiness, unoffended with sin, careless about His laws, or partial towards His subjects. No, not one. What, then, is it that has effected such a remarkable difference between God's relation to man, and His relation to ruined angels? IT IS THE ATONEMENT. The atonement has completely removed every obstacle arising out of His character, as a holy and just Governor, that could possibly stand between us and salvation. It has not pardoned any, it has not justified any, it has not redeemed any, it has not reconciled any, it has not glorified any; but it has removed all obstacles of government standing between us and the enjoyment of those blessings – so that if we be not pardoned, justified, redeemed, reconciled, and ultimately glorified, we have ourselves, and ourselves only, to blame. It is in this sense that Jesus is a 'mediator between God and men'; it is in this sense that He is a 'propitiation' for our sins; it is in this sense that He has 'made an end of sins' (Dan. 9:24), 'and put them away'

(Heb. 9:26). They no longer exist as a *legal* barrier between us and salvation.

SECT. 5. It may be of importance to consider for a little, in what manner Jesus has effected this remarkable change in our relation toward God, and the claims of His Law. It was by His 'obedience unto death' in our behalf (Phil. 2:8). His 'obedience unto death', or His 'righteousness', as it is generally termed at once in the Old and New Testaments, constitutes the matter or substance of the atonement. By His 'righteousness' we are to understand both what He did and what He suffered – His entire compliance with the precepts and penalty of the Law. Jesus, being Himself God, was above the Law. The Law was made by Him, and was made for creatures, and for creatures alone. If all men had obeyed all its precepts for ever, the Law would have been honoured, and God would have shown His good pleasure, by rewarding us with 'everlasting life'. Since all men have broken its precepts, it would still have been fully honoured, as it is in the place of perdition, had God vindicated His regard for it by our everlasting destruction. It was because His Law must be honoured and vindicated, that our state was almost remediless, and our prospects almost darkened with everlasting despair.* How could the Law-giving God be just, and yet the Law-breaking man be saved? Here was the mighty problem that Divinity resolved. 'The Word became flesh,' God became incarnate. Though Himself the Lawgiver, He 'was made under the law'; and surely His obedience to its precepts is ten thousand times more honouring to its purity, and goodness, and equity, than would have been the eternal compliance with its injunctions of the whole human race. Not only did Jesus thus magnify the Law by obeying its precepts, He also became 'obedient unto death', although He never merited death by any personal breach of its requirements. 'He became a curse for us sinners', because we had desecrated the Law's majesty, and tarnished its heavenly holiness; and He surely thus showed His own and His Father's ineffable esteem for its righteousness and purity; their unutterable detestation of SIN 'its transgression'; and their unwavering determination to maintain its honour unsullied, and its efficacy unmaimed – ten thousand times more convincingly than could have been demonstrated by the everlasting perdition of

---

* See the profound and invaluable dissertation of Jonathan Edwards 'On the Necessity and Reasonableness of the Christian Doctrine of Satisfaction for Sin.'

the whole rebellious world. The Law is thus 'magnified and made honourable', by the 'obedience unto death' of the holy Lawgiver in our room. This was never done for angels; but it was done, O wonder! Wonder! For sinners of mankind. Sinner, it was done for you. Seeing, then, that the only reason why God cannot admit fallen angels to the enjoyment of His favour, is the imperious moral necessity under which His own holiness lays Him to vindicate the honour of His insulted Law; and seeing that this obstacle, in the case of man, is entirely removed, here we have an expedient by which mankind-sinners may be pardoned, justified, redeemed, reconciled, and glorified, whilst God's government is safe, and His glory is untarnished. As Jesus suffered what in its effects upon the Divine moral government is assuredly more than equivalent to our own personal endurance of the full punishment of our sins, it may, with propriety, be said, that our sins have been answered for by Him. 'The chastisement of our peace was upon Him' (Isa. 53:5). It is in this sense that He 'bare our sins in His own body on the tree' (1 Pet. 2:24), and 'was wounded for our transgressions' (Isa. 53:5). Every legal obstacle between us and their pardon was by Him completely abolished (Isa. 1:18).

SECT. 6. But now if you be an unbeliever, your sins, though thus 'borne' by Christ; though thus fully and freely atoned for by His 'precious blood,' are yet unpardoned, and you yourself are yet unjustified, unredeemed, unreconciled to God. Obstacles to your salvation which you yourself could never have surmounted have indeed been removed; but one other obstacle still remains. That obstacle is not on God's part, it is on your own part; it arises not out of the claims of God's government, but out of the hardness and 'desperate wickedness' of your own heart; it is no barrier without you, it is within you: it is your UNBELIEF. The only reason why you are not pardoned, justified, redeemed, reconciled, is this – you do not believe that God does love you, that God does desire your salvation, that Jesus did die for you, and made a complete satisfaction for your sins. God's great end with regard to you is to secure, not so much your pardon as your purification; not so much your safety as your sanctification. Your pardon and safety are valuable only as means to your sanctification. 'This is the will of God, even your sanctification' (1 Thess. 4:3). His wish is, that we should be 'holy and without blame before Him in love' (Eph. 1:4). It is because heathens are unholy, and not because their sins are unatoned for, that they are not saved. It is because unbelievers are unsanctified, as long as they refuse to believe THE ONLY TRUTH THAT CAN MELT AND CHANGE THE HEART, that God has made it essential to our salvation that we should believe His love to us in providing for our sins a complete atonement. Unbeliever, this unbelief of yours is now the only barrier between you and immediate salvation. O then, will you not be persuaded, even by God Himself, that He did 'so love' *you*, as a part of 'the world' which He loved, that He gave His own Son to die for you? Will you not believe that that Son 'put away your sin'? Will you not believe that in Him eternal life is given unto you (1 Jn 5:11)? All this is true, because the God of truth asserts it, whether you will believe it or not; and now God is just WAITING for you to credit his testimony regarding it, that He may pardon, justify, redeem, and reconcile you.

SECT. 7. Do not suppose that you have to do anything whatsoever, but believe God, and take Him at His word, in order to secure your salvation. You can do nothing else. Perhaps, like many others, you may be wishing to make yourself a *little better* before you can persuade yourself that God does love you, and will be willing to pardon you. If you are, it is a vain wish. You never can be better before you be pardoned and safe; and even though you could, your betterness could no more help to bring you nearer pardon than would your sins. You never will be, by the space of one atom, nearer pardon than you are at this moment, till you become a believer. There is nothing in the universe but the blood of Jesus that has any tendency to save your soul; and as that blood is already shed, and shed for you, there is nothing in the universe that can make you one iota better qualified to be saved by it than you are at this moment. 'How, then', you may be inclined to ask, 'am I to get, and get this moment, the benefit of this blood?' Simply by believing that it was poured out for *you*, that it is an ample atonement for your guilt, and a clear demonstration of God's 'unspeakable love' to your soul. Believe this, and pardon, justification, redemption, reconciliation, everlasting life, are YOURS (Jn 3:36).

SECT. 8. Perhaps you are still hanging off, and inclined, from very shame of yourself, to keep away from immediately taking salvation, 'laying hold on eternal life', and calling Jesus your Saviour. Perhaps you are saying 'O, I abhor myself; I tremble, I am such a monster of iniquity; surely there is no devil in the place of woe so black with sin as I.' No, sinner, there is not; no devil in the place of woe ever rejected a Saviour, as you have done, and trod His blood as an unholy thing under foot like you. But 'unto *you* is the word of salvation sent'. The propitiation was for you. The Law was 'magnified and made honourable' for you. A 'righteousness' was wrought out, and woven from head to foot with the blood-dyed threads of the Saviour's sufferings, for you. Do you believe it? Then you will feel assured that you have got all you were needing, as a dying and a second-death deserving criminal. Is it thus that you feel? Suppose that, instead of being born and reared in an enlightened country, a libraried land, where every man either has, or may have, a Bible of his own, and ability to read it; suppose that, instead of this, you were a heathen in the centre of some remote island that had never been gladdened by the 'joyful sound'; suppose that, in these circumstances, you had, from the light of nature and the work of God's Spirit in your conscience, come to see that you were a 'grievous sinner' in the sight of the righteous Governor of the world; suppose that you had also arrived at the conclusion that sin must be punished, because God is just – you would be in despair, and your bosom would become the home of the direst forebodings of unutterable woe. 'Ah! Could nothing be done by which I might be saved?' we suppose to be your frequent and your bitter ejaculation. Suppose that at this crisis a missionary should arrive in your country, and come forward and proclaim in your wondering ears 'Good news for you, heathens! I bring you good news.' 'What! News for me?' you would say. 'Yes, for you, O man! Here is something new, and no less wonderful than new, and no more new and wonderful than true. God foresaw that you were to become vile and depraved; He foresaw that you could do nothing to extricate yourself from the ruin in which you are almost already ensnared; He pitied you; aye, even you; He sent His own Divine Son into the world to obey the Law which you have broken, to bear all the penalty which you have incurred; and now God is satisfied as your Governor, and only waits that you should believe, that you may live.' 'Believe it! Ah, would to heaven that it were a truth; but it is quite incredible. Tell me of high mountains becoming plains; tell me of low valleys becoming mountains; tell me of darkness becoming light, and of light becoming darkness; but tantalise me not by telling me that Divinity became man to die for ME!' 'Here', says the man of God, 'is God's own handwriting on the matter. I carry in my hand a missive He handed to me from heaven; it is the Bible.' 'He is True, He is Truth. Is that indeed His own written word? and does it indeed tell to me what you say?' 'O man, yes it does; hear what it says while I read: "Christ died for our sins (that is, for your sins and my sins), according to the Scriptures" (1 Cor. 15:3). "This is the record that God hath given to us (that is, to you and to me) eternal life, and this life is in His Son" (1 John 5:11).' 'Ah, then, thou messenger of glad tidings, if this be all true, my unbelief I give to the winds, my fears I cast behind my back, and like a little child I will take my Father at His word, and seeing He has made a gift to me of everlasting life, I accept it, and I feel as if never more shall I be afraid of everlasting death.' O sinner, do you feel thus? We do beseech you, come now, NOW, to the gospel, as if you had never heard of it before; become 'a fool,' that you may be 'wise unto salvation.' O, believe the gospel and live! Your unbelief is now the only possible obstacle between you and salvation. Wait not for holy love; wait not for fervent prayers; wait not for deeper convictions; wait not for anything more than what you have at this moment within your reach. God by His Spirit calls you now. Only believe God's own record, that He 'hath given to us eternal life and this life is in His Son.' Yes, believe this and be saved, and rest assured that all that is needed for bliss will be granted unto you according to His promises, which are yea and amen in Christ Jesus.

Notes

Note A, p. 32.

See 'The Judgment of the late Archbishop of Armagh and Primate of Ireland, of the true Intent and Extent of Christ's death and Satisfaction on the Cross,' p. 4. In another place, p. 32, he says, 'Now, the *general* satisfaction of Christ, which was the first act of His *priestly* office, prepares the way for God's mercy, by making the sins of all mankind *pardonable,* the interposition of any bar from God's justice notwithstanding, and so puts the sons of men only in a *possibility* of being justified, a thing denied to the nature of fallen angels, which the Son was not pleased to assume; but the *special application* of this satisfaction vouchsafed by Christ unto those persons only whom the Father 'hath given Him out of the world,' which *is* an appendant, or appertaineth to the *second* act of His priesthood, *viz.*, *His intercession, procureth* an actual discharge from God's anger, and maketh justification, which before was a part of our *possibility* to be a part of our present *possession.*' This little work of the venerable Archbishop is one of the best old books on the universality of the atonement. It is a masterpiece. Its author was indeed a wonderful man. His personal piety seems to have been deep and enlightened; and as to his erudition, the most competent judges speak in the most glowing terms. He is styled by Morus, 'a breathing library' (*Bibliotheca spirans*). Selden said of him, he was 'a man of great piety, singular judgment, learned to a miracle'; and Dr Prideaux calls him 'solidae eruditionis et totius antiquitatis Gazophylacium,' that is, 'the magazine of solid learning and of all antiquity.' (See Dr Bernard's *Life and Death of Dr James Usher.*)

NOTE B, P. 42.

The whole passage in Romans 3:24, runs thus, 'Through the redemption that is in Christ Jesus.' If there be any passage in the Bible where 'redemption' might mean something else than *actual deliverance,* this would be it. Some might not unnaturally be inclined to suppose that the word here denotes *the price of deliverance.* Here also, however, it must have its invariable meaning, and the clause must be explained in the manner that it is explained in the text. To show that we are not forcing an unnatural signification upon the term in this place, it may not be improper to subjoin the remarks of some of the standard expositors upon the clause in question. By these remarks (most of them made by men who held the limited atonement) the reader will perceive that the word redemption does not mean *the price of deliverance,* but the *actual deliverance procured by the price.*

Calvin says, 'Christus, vices nostras subeundo, tyrannide mortis, qua tenebamur captivi, nos *liberavit.*' J.A. Turretin says, 'Redemptio, vel *liberatio* in genere, soluto pretio hand exiguo.' Wilson says, *'The redemption which is in Christ,* by which is meant a *delivery* from sin and misery, by the merit and power of Christ's blood shed.' J. Brown of Wamphray says, 'That spiritual redemption which was by price, whereby we were *freed* from guilt, the curse of God, the law, Satan, and death.' Mortis says, 'Liberatio a malo, quod e peccato oritur, de quo malo multa sunt dicta ante.' – Conf. Eph. 1:7, i.e., aliis verbis, venia peccati.' Haldane says, 'Redemption signifies in Scripture *deliverance* by price, as that of slaves, or prisoners, or persons condemned, when they are *delivered* from slavery, captivity, or death, by means of a ransom. In this acceptation the word is used here.' Moses Stuart says, 'Λυτροω and

$απολυτροω$ both mean *to pay the price of ransom*: $απολυτροω$ is somewhat *intensive*, and = *pay off*. Accordingly $λυτροσις$ and $απολυτρωσις$ mean (1) *The act of paying this price*; and (2) The consequences of this act, *viz.*, *the redemption* which follows it. In this way the idea of $απολυτρωσις$ comes at times to be merely a generic one, i.e., *liberation, deliverance. Της εν Χριστω Ιησου* designates the author of our redemption or liberation, *viz.*, Him who paid the ransom, and procured our freedom, when we were the slaves and captives of sin and Satan, and exposed to the wrath of God (1:18). The sequel defines more exactly what the writer understands by $απολυτρωσεως$ in this place.' Barnes says, 'The word here denotes that *deliverance* from sin and from the evil consequences of sin, which has been effected by the offering of Jesus Christ as a propitiation.' Hodge says, 'Redemption, when applied to the work of Christ, as effecting our deliverance from the punishment of sin, *is always taken in its proper sense* DELIVERANCE effected by the payment of a ransom.' We might go on to quote the opinions of many other commentators, but what we have already transcribed is certainly sufficient for our purpose. When believers, then, are said by the apostle to be 'justified through the redemption that is in Christ

Jesus,' the meaning of the expression must be, that they are 'judicially treated by God as if righteous, in consequence of having received from Christ, by faith, deliverance from the curse of the law.'

There is another passage in which the word may not unnaturally by English readers be confounded with the atonement, or the price of deliverance; we refer to Hebrews 9:15. 'For this cause Christ is the mediator of the new testament, that by means of death, for the redemption of the transgressions that were under the first testament, they which are called might receive the promise of eternal inheritance.' Here the phrase translated 'the redemption of the transgressions,' should have been rendered, 'the redemption (or deliverance) from the transgressions.' It is 'transgressors', and not 'transgressions,' that can be said to be 'redeemed'. The original expression bears the rendering we have given, as will be admitted by all who understand the influence which the Greek writers frequently attribute to the preposition in composition. The apostle means that Christ's death was designed to 'deliver transgressors from the punishment of their transgressions committed under (or *against*, so Syriac version, Owen, Pierce, *&c.*) the first covenant, in order that the called might, by consequence (that is, after, and in consequence of, their redemption), receive the promised eternal inheritance.' In looking into the old Peschito version, we perceive that it supports this interpretation. Literally translated it runs thus: 'Therefore is He made the mediator of the new covenant, that by His death He might be redemption to those who had transgressed the first covenant, that they who are called to the eternal inheritance might receive the promise.' Dr Owen, in his commentary on the place, remarks: 'The redemption of transgressions is the deliverance of the transgressors from all the evils they are subject unto on their account, by the payment of a satisfactory price'; and a little further on he says, 'Here it must answer *the purging of conscience by the blood of Christ*' (see v. 14). Of whomsoever the apostle is speaking, he evidently regards them as *not yet* having entered upon the possession of the promised inheritance, and he assumes that it was necessary that they should *first* be delivered from their transgressions. The word redemption, then, here also, as everywhere else, denotes *actual deliverance*. This, moreover, is the only meaning of the term which is given by the standard New

Testament lexicographers, as, for example, Leigh, Pasor, Schoettgen, Krebsius, Schleusner, Robinson, &c.